THIS LAND CALLED AMERICA: NEW YORK

CREATIVE EDUCATION

Published by Creative Education
P.O. Box 227, Mankato, Minnesota 56002
Creative Education is an imprint of The Creative Company
www.thecreativecompany.us

Design by Blue Design (www.bluedes.com)
Art direction by Rita Marshall
Book production by The Design Lab
Printed in the United States of America

Photographs by Alamy (Classic Image, Content Mine International, Richard
Levine, North Wind Picture Archives, Stock Montage, Inc.), Corbis (Alan
Schein Photography, Bettmann, Stefano Bianchetti, Gaetano, Hulton-Deutsch
Collection, The Mariners' Museum, Daniel Mirer, David Muench, Bo Zaun-
ders), Dreamstime (Familyfotographer, Roxpix 2007), Getty Images (Hulton
Archive, Curt Maas, J. Meric, MPI, Jake Rajs, Harald Sund), iStockphoto
(Vishwanatha Srinivasan)

Library of Congress Cataloging-in-Publication Data
Tougas, Joe.
New York / by Joe Tougas.
p. cm. — (This land called America)
Includes bibliographical references and index.
ISBN 978-1-58341-785-0
1. New York (State)—Juvenile literature. I. Title. II. Series.
F119.3.T68 2009
974.7—dc22   2008009514

First Edition
9 8 7 6 5 4 3 2 1

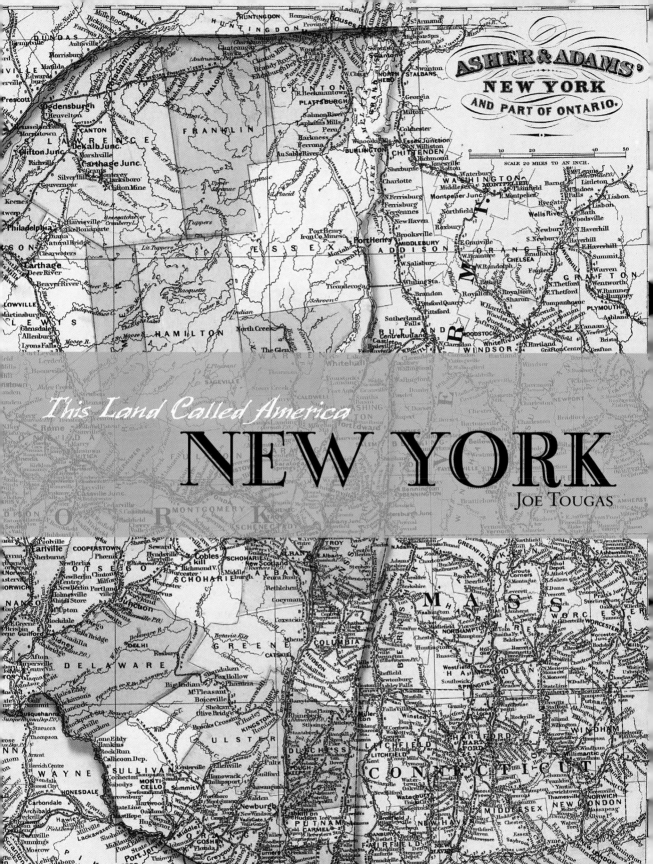

This Land Called America

NEW YORK

Joe Tougas

New York

JOE TOUGAS

THE SUN HAS NOT YET COME UP IN NEWPORT, NEW YORK, WHEN A DAIRY FARMER WALKS OUT INTO THE COOL, DARK MORNING AND HEADS FOR HIS MILKING BARN. FROM THE THICK STAND OF NORTHERN WHITE CEDAR TREES NEARBY, HE CAN HEAR CHICKADEES AND EASTERN BLUEBIRDS START THEIR MORNING SONGS. IN THE BARN, ROWS OF BLACK-AND-WHITE HOLSTEIN COWS ARE STANDING IN THEIR STALLS, PATIENTLY WAITING TO BE MILKED. THE FARMER ATTACHES ONE OF HIS MILKING MACHINES TO THE COWS' UDDERS. WITH A LOUD "SHHH" SOUND, THE MACHINE BEGINS TO COLLECT MILK. IT'S THE BEGINNING OF ANOTHER BUSY MORNING IN NORTHERN NEW YORK.

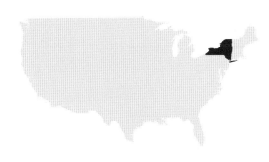

YEAR

1524 Italian explorer Giovanni da Verrazano discovers New York Bay.

EVENT

A New Home

THE FIRST PEOPLE TO LIVE IN WHAT IS NOW NEW YORK
WERE AMERICAN INDIANS. THE ALGONQUIN LIVED IN
THE SOUTHERN PART OF THE REGION, AND THE MORE
POWERFUL IROQUOIS WERE SPREAD THROUGHOUT THE
REST OF THE AREA. BOTH GROUPS SURVIVED BY HUNTING
DEER, ELK, MOOSE, BEARS, AND WILD TURKEYS.

The first European to reach the area was probably an Italian named Giovanni da Verrazano. He is believed to have sailed his ship into lower New York Bay in 1524. French and Spanish explorers followed and set up successful fur trades with the American Indians. But they did not settle there. In 1609, the Dutch sent Englishman Henry Hudson to find a shorter route to Asia. As part of his search, he sailed into New York Bay and up the waterway now called the Hudson River.

Eventually, Dutch settlers took over the land. In 1613, Dutch explorer Adriaen Block anchored his boat off an island the Indians called *Manahatta*, or "Island of the Hills." The ship caught fire, and friendly Indians helped Block and his men build homes. They were the first white people to live in what later became New York City.

Before Adriaen Block discovered the Indians living in longhouses on Manhattan Island (opposite), Henry Hudson encountered other tribes (above).

YEAR

1609   Englishman Henry Hudson reaches New York Bay and sails up the river now named after him.

EVENT

- 7 -

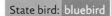
State bird: bluebird

Block continued to explore the area, and word of his travels led the Netherlands to claim much of the region as its own. The Dutch called the land New Netherland. It included parts of the present-day states of New York, New Jersey, Connecticut, and Delaware. The settlement on Manahatta Island was given the name New Amsterdam.

By 1640, New Amsterdam's population numbered about 500. The Dutch enjoyed mingling with people from other cultures, so the colony of New Netherland attracted people of many different nationalities. New Amsterdam in particular became a "melting pot" of different races and religions.

In 1664, the English seized the colony by military force. They changed New Netherland's name to New York, after the Duke of York in England. The town of New Amsterdam was renamed New York City.

By 1750, England ruled the 13 colonies of eastern North America. But the Revolutionary War between England and the colonies, which lasted from 1775 to 1783, led to American independence and the creation of the United States. New York proved to be an important battleground during the war, especially after the English captured New York City in 1776. New York became the 11th state on July 26, 1788. From 1785 to 1790, New York City was America's capital, and its first president, George Washington, lived there.

The colonies joined forces to form the Continental Army, which was also known as "Washington's Army."

YEAR

1613   The first white settlers from the Netherlands establish homes in the colony they call New Netherland.

EVENT

- 9 -

The Civil War volunteers who fought for the North were organized into units such as the 12th New York Infantry.

Fewer than 30 years after the end of the Revolutionary War, New York became the site of many battles during the War of 1812. This two-year war between the U.S. and England was fought over military and trade practices. New York was also involved in the U.S. Civil War, which began in 1861 and was fought largely over the issue of slavery. New York sided with the Northern, anti-slavery states against the Southern, pro-slavery states. By the time the war ended in 1865, 50,000 New Yorkers had died in the fighting.

Despite the state's Civil War losses, New York's population boomed in the late 1800s. European immigrants sailed across the Atlantic Ocean to America by the thousands. By 1900, more than seven million people from around the world had decided to call New York home.

Even a foggy glimpse of the Statue of Liberty gave new immigrants hope in the late 1800s and early 1900s.

YEAR

1664   New Netherland becomes an English colony and is renamed New York.

EVENT

Neighbors and Lakes

New York is in the northeastern part of the U.S. It is bordered by Quebec, Canada, and Lake Ontario to the north. To the east are Vermont, Massachusetts, and Connecticut. New Jersey and Pennsylvania border the state to the south, and Pennsylvania, Lake Erie, and Ontario, Canada, lie to the west.

For many who do not live in New York, it is hard to think of it as a state where forests cover the majority of the land. But outside of New York City, there are many thick, hilly forests of maple, birch, spruce, and white pine. White-tailed deer, foxes, raccoons, and other wildlife run through the forests.

Majestic mountain ranges also tower over parts of New York. The Catskills can be found in the southeast, and the Adirondacks cover most of the northeast. Mount Marcy, the highest mountain in the Adirondacks, is also New York's highest point, at 5,344 feet (1,629 m).

New York has many notable bodies of water. The waves of the Atlantic Ocean wash against the state's southeastern corner. In the west, the Great Lakes of Erie and Ontario separate New York from Canada and are connected by the Niagara River. The three stunning, powerful waterfalls that make up Niagara Falls are located about 15 miles (25 km) from the river's end at Lake Ontario.

From the calmness of Heart Lake in the Adirondacks (opposite) to the powerful display of Niagara Falls (above), New York has no shortage of scenery.

YEAR

1725   The colony's first newspaper, the *New York Gazette,* is published in New York City.

EVENT

New York's land supports many farms. In fact, 25 percent of the state's land is used for farming. New York is one of the largest dairy producers in the country. An estimated 10,000 dairy farms produce nearly 1.4 billion gallons (5.3 billion l) of milk per year. Only Wisconsin and California produce more milk.

Although more than half of New York's farming profits come from milk sales, many fruits, vegetables, and grains are also grown across the state. Apple orchards can be found throughout New York, especially in the north. The state produces about 25,000 bushels of apples a year, making it the second-largest apple producer in the U.S. Other crops grown in New York include cabbage, corn, onions, oats, and wheat. New York's farms also produce livestock, poultry, and eggs.

Visitors to western New York can see history preserved at Knox Farm State Park (above) or travel east and pick apples in one of the state's many orchards in the Hudson Valley (opposite).

1777   The American colonists' victory at Saratoga is a turning point in the Revolutionary War against England.

Winters in New York can be harsh, and bad snowstorms can stop traffic even in New York City.

Much of New York's land is also mined for oil and gas. More than 75,000 wells have been drilled in the state since the late 1800s, and about 14,000 still operate today. Oil, gas, and salt mining generate about $500 million in state revenue each year.

New York's summers are mild. Temperatures usually hold steady around 66 °F (19 °C) in the Adirondacks and average 74 °F (23 °C) in the southeast. In the winter, temperatures that are consistently below freezing cause lakes and some rivers in the central and northern areas to freeze.

The Catskills and Adirondacks get more snow than the rest of the state. Annual snowfall averages in the Adirondacks range from 60 to more than 140 inches (150–355 cm), with the higher amounts being recorded closer to Lake Ontario. The Catskills usually see 60 to 100 inches (150–255 cm) of snow a year. In New York City, yearly snowfall usually totals about 29 inches (74 cm), but the city occasionally gets hit hard with winter storms. On February 12, 2006, a winter storm dumped a record 27 inches (69 cm) of snow on the metropolis.

Dry mining for salt takes place in large underground caverns and uses vehicles with wide cutting tools.

Snowed-in taxicab

New Yorkers

FOR MANY YEARS, PEOPLE WHO CAME TO AMERICA FROM OTHER COUNTRIES LANDED IN NEW YORK CITY. THE STATUE OF LIBERTY, WHICH WAS GIVEN TO NEW YORK BY THE FRENCH AND ERECTED IN 1886, SERVED AS A SYMBOL OF THE COUNTRY'S ACCEPTANCE OF PEOPLE FROM OTHER COUNTRIES. THE STATUE STILL STANDS

on Liberty Island next to Ellis Island, where, between 1892 and 1954, newly arrived citizens would register to live in America. By the time Ellis Island's immigrant station closed, it had welcomed more than 12 million people to the U.S.

Many of the people who first landed in New York City decided to stay there. As a result, the city is a mix of nationalities and cultures. African Americans make up 26 percent of the city's population, and Hispanics make up 27 percent. Almost one million Jews also call New York City home. This is the greatest number of Jews in any area outside of Israel. The city's Chinese population continues to grow as well. There are

The Statue of Liberty was sculpted in France (opposite) before it was sent to the U.S. and put together to welcome immigrants to the country (above).

YEAR

1789   George Washington is sworn in as the first U.S. president in New York.

EVENT

- *19* -

As an abolitionist, native New Yorker Julia Ward Howe was opposed to slavery.

clusters of Irish, Italian, Polish, German, and French people throughout the city, too. Outside of New York City, which contains almost half of New York's population, the state is made up mostly of people of European heritage.

Among those who have called New York home have been many great leaders and legends. One of the most famous early female leaders was Julia Ward Howe. Known first for her writing talent (as author of the poem "Battle Hymn of the Republic"), Howe became an outspoken advocate for women's right to vote during the late 1800s. However, she died 10 years before the U.S. Congress granted that right to all women in 1920.

Photography teacher Lewis Hine documented many immigrants' arrivals at Ellis Island.

YEAR

1812 New York is the site of many battles during the War of 1812.

EVENT

- 20 -

A legend of a different sort also came from New York. Lou Gehrig, one of baseball's greatest and most beloved players, was born in New York City in 1903. He played for the New York Yankees from 1923 to 1939 and hit 493 home runs during his 16-year career. One of Gehrig's teammates (until 1935) was the famed "Sultan of Swat," Babe Ruth.

Lou Gehrig (left) and Babe Ruth (right) were big stars and competitive teammates.

Today, New York City is the center of much of the world's business. Many people around the world buy stocks, or shares of a company's ownership. They hope that as time goes by, the company will do well, and the shares will become more valuable. New York City's business district on Wall Street is where stocks are traded and their values change from day to day. Many major worldwide banks and corporations also have their headquarters in the city's business district.

Inside the New York Stock Exchange on Wall Street are rooms where stocks are traded.

YEAR

1865   The Civil War ends; about 50,000 soldiers from New York have been killed during the war.

EVENT

N

ew York City is also the publishing center of the country. Book companies such as HarperCollins and Simon & Schuster publish books that are read worldwide. News magazines such as *Time* and *Newsweek* are published in New York City, as are national newspapers such as *The New York Times* and *USA Today*. The city has always been a place that nurtures writers. New York gave the world "America's Poet," Walt Whitman. His 1855 book of poetry, *Leaves of Grass,* is still considered a classic.

Both within and outside of New York City, many people work in factories. New York is one of America's largest producers of medical devices, cameras, and clothes. In addition, the state's 36,000 farms bring in more than $3 billion in annual revenue.

Founded four years before poet Walt Whitman's (opposite) Leaves of Grass *was published,* The New York Times *(above) remains one of the country's most respected newspapers.*

Center of So Much

FROM ITS QUIET MOUNTAIN RETREATS TO THE FAST-PACED BUSTLE OF NEW YORK CITY, NEW YORK HAS SOMETHING FOR EVERYONE. MANY ARTISTS, MUSICIANS, ACTORS, AND WRITERS COME FROM AROUND THE WORLD TO LIVE IN NEW YORK CITY. NEW YORK HAS BEEN A CENTER OF THE MODERN ART WORLD SINCE THE MID-20TH CENTURY, WHEN ARTISTS THERE BEGAN TO MOVE AWAY FROM THE CLASSIC

styles of art that had come from Europe. In 1929, the Museum of Modern Art was built to exhibit new, experimental styles of art such as cubism. Today, visitors from around the world tour the museum's collections.

The 1933 version of King Kong *was known for its early innovations in special effects and animation.*

People who want to be professional actors also come to New York City. They hope to find a role on Broadway, a district where numerous theaters stage great plays and musicals. Broadway theaters offer some of the best entertainment in the world.

Many movies are also filmed in New York City, and they have made the city's landmarks famous. A giant ape first climbed the Empire State Building in the 1933 movie *King Kong*. The New York Stock Exchange was a setting in 1987's *Wall Street*. Many movies also show people ice skating at Rockefeller Center in the heart of midtown New York.

One of the most-filmed locations in the city is also one of its most popular attractions: Central Park. The trees, lawns, and walking paths of this 840-acre (340 ha) park are nestled among Manhattan's skyscrapers. The park offers a calm setting in a city that is busy with movement, traffic, and noise.

Times Square is a bustling scene every night, but it is especially crowded on New Year's Eve.

YEAR
1939   New York hosts a World's Fair, with more than 44 million people in attendance.
EVENT

- 27 -

This bustling city was the location of a very dark chapter in America's recent history. New York was a target of the attacks on September 11, 2001, when terrorists hijacked passenger airplanes and flew two of them into the twin towers of the World Trade Center. The towers collapsed, and nearly 3,000 people were killed. The 1,776-foot-tall (541 m) Freedom Tower memorial will stand on the site of the former World Trade Center by 2012.

Away from the skyscrapers of New York City, outdoor enthusiasts find plenty to do in New York. Lake Placid, two-time home of the Winter Olympics in 1932 and 1980, hosts a bobsled and luge competition nearly every weekend throughout the winter months. Ski jumping competitions are held there in early January and mid-March.

Professional sports are also popular in New York. Today, there are 13 professional sports teams in the state, including the Yankees and Mets in baseball and the Buffalo Bills, New York Giants, and New York Jets in football. The New York Rangers, Buffalo Sabres, and New York Islanders play hockey. The state's men's basketball team is the Knicks and the women's team is the Liberty.

Six months after the World Trade Center was attacked, a light memorial was beamed into the night sky.

YEAR

1952   The United Nations' headquarters is built in New York City.

EVENT

QUICK FACTS

Population: 19,297,729

Largest City: New York City (pop. 8,274,527)

Capital: Albany

Entered the union: July 26, 1788

Nickname: Empire State

State flower: rose

State bird: bluebird

Size: 54,556 sq mi (141,299 sq km)—27th-biggest in U.S.

Major industries: agriculture, manufacturing, finance, publishing

From the excitement of a Yankees ballgame to the peace of an Adirondacks canoeing trip, New York is a state that offers the best of both urban and natural worlds. With its ever-growing role as a place for serious business and exciting art, New York City will continue to draw attention and activity from around the world. Meanwhile, greater New York will continue to serve as a place of beauty, interesting history, and a calmer lifestyle—a place of escape for both tourists and New Yorkers looking for a change of pace.

YEAR	
2001	Terrorists attack the twin towers of the World Trade Center, killing nearly 3,000 people.

EVENT

BIBLIOGRAPHY

Allen, Leslie. *Liberty: The Statue and the American Dream*. New York: Statue of Liberty-Ellis Island Foundation with the cooperation of the National Geographic Society, 1985.

Atkinson, Brooks. *Broadway*. New York: Macmillan, 1970.

Dunsmore, Renate. "Hiking in New York State's Adirondack Mountains." Onondaga County Public Library. http://www.onlib.org/website/pathfinders/hiking.htm.

Kammen, Michael. *Colonial New York: A History*. New York: Charles Scribner's Sons, 1975.

Langguth, A. J. *Union 1812: The Americans Who Fought the Second War of Independence*. New York: Simon and Schuster, 2006.

INDEX